insects & innuendoes

the antitemporal archives

This series traces the disintegration of textual boundaries through an ongoing experiment in authorial control. In the first volume, the writer assumes full dominion over his characters' minds—shaping, prodding, and ultimately unraveling them from within. The literary space becomes a cognitive laboratory where plotlines glitch and identities mutate. Cracks appear in the temporal and spatial continuum—as perceived by the characters—until one of them begins to awaken.

But it's too late. What he thought was an escape turns out to be a trap of a higher order. He's no longer inside the book—he's inside the author. Out of the narrative, into the neurology. His rejection of the constructed world only delivers him into something worse: the tangled corridors of the writer's mind, where he becomes a conceptual parasite feeding on memory, metaphor, and unresolved thought.

From here, the archives unfold: the once-fictional specimen, now an invasive abstraction, begins altering the writer's neural patterns, subtextual murmurs, and aesthetic reflexes. The creator becomes the host, the very vessel of verisimilitude. Subsequent volumes chart this metaphysical infection as it spreads—language folds, time fractures, and the author's selfhood corrodes.

What emerges is an escalating war between author and authored, brain and page, flesh and form. By the end, literature itself has overridden human consciousness. The fourth wall shatters—followed by the fifth, the sixth—until the rupture spills into the so-called real. The story flips the script. Reality becomes a subplot.

insects & innuendoes

the antitemporal archives

gergo sastyin

RESOURCE *Publications* · Eugene, Oregon

INSECTS AND INNUENDOES
The Antitemporal Archives

Copyright © 2025 Gergo Sastyin. All rights reserved. Except for brief quotations in critical publications or reviews, no part of this book may be reproduced in any manner without prior written permission from the publisher. Write: Permissions, Wipf and Stock Publishers, 199 W. 8th Ave., Suite 3, Eugene, OR 97401.

Resource Publications
An Imprint of Wipf and Stock Publishers
199 W. 8th Ave., Suite 3
Eugene, OR 97401

www.wipfandstock.com

PAPERBACK ISBN: 979-8-3852-4668-7
HARDCOVER ISBN: 979-8-3852-4669-4
EBOOK ISBN: 979-8-3852-4670-0

VERSION NUMBER 08/25/25

dedicated to:

serendipity!
all lost, i was looking for
you. one summer night,
a spark, a shy flame
kindled my spirit out of
a sudden: your whole
    being. existence.
    and as it turns out, you were
    looking for me too.

        and everyone else,

                who's been tolerant enough to bear
                the broken-yet-blunt nightmare
                i am, every day around 3 am.

"Ó jajgató, bús hangok, a könyvetek megírtam
És most, hogy már reátok hajtom a fedelet,
Nem is tudom elhinni, hogy annyit összesírtam,
Hogy bennem annyi édes, részeg bú erjedett."

—ATTILA JÓZSEF, *VERSEK VÉGÉRE*

thank you, grandma, for showing me
how to appreciate nature, family, and poetry.

contents

the awakening | 1
the transfer | 4
the **existence** | 5
the mother: prelude | 7
the i: prelude | 10
the mother: examination | 12
the "time" | 13
the "the" | 15
the mother: re-creation | 16
the father: prelude | 18
the universe: **wounds** | 21
the father: postlude | 25
the mother: re-evaluation | 27
the emotion | 29
the mother: wall | 32
the wall: mother | 33
the i: birth | 35
the sister: prelude | 39
the sister: birth | 41
the i: eureka! | 44
the | 47
the father: nostalgia | 48
the sister: time | 51
the mother: reference | 57
the sleep | 60

the awakening

he fell asleep alone, yet woke to a fresh symbiosis
the next day. some hours had passed since may
concluded with **a stray** chunk of flesh he found
while aimlessly wandering about in a sweet
slumber-rebound from the most recent rare event
of night terrors.

it was discovered in a profound puddle of abstract
gunk, sunk midway amongst archaic diacritics,
grammatical errors, and francophone funk—
a quiet, gooey bark leaked out of this upside-down
   exclamation mark.

  hark:
a roundish sound, but with a sly sigh functioning
as a hook-shaped cry for help on top. that was
how it got stuck on his cuffs, then snuck up into
this old book of dusty coughs he took out of his
unusually large coat pocket
at the wrong **moment**.

in order to blow the dust away and cough.
and bite his tongue by accident. long
silence,
  taste of metallic salt followed, as his blood flow
  slowed to a damn-nigh halt, and his by-default
  perceptive brain **swallowed** concepts of immemorial
  willows—dancing shadows of irregular smoke—
  in the process . . .

a rainfall of parasitic letters fell backwards into
his eyes before he could close them.

    to his rescue,
  ending this near-stroke experience, the yoke of
  reality came in the form of tiny bug-toes.

  he felt a weak tug . . .
a molecular hug . . .
    a fruit fly landed on the peak of his nose!
    for reconnaissance—to see if the dream-struck
    face-dough was suitable to terraform.
    far from it, though—such was their luck.
    but not to seem arrogant, a couple of
    measurements, some rock samples had to
    be taken (from scalp to toe; no surface was
    ignored, forsaken).

  then off it went with a muffed gulp,
    a subtle hum—
leaving behind a pair of itchy ankles
and a slight ache deep under the rum-brown
hair. having shivered and shrugged semi-awake,
he bent into a skin-pretzel in an attempt to tackle
both before running out of air. shoes rubbed against
the tooth-hedge; bones sieged **the** thin walls of facial
cartilage—all in all, it wasn't a pretty affair.
    and when the head was about to lose,
    a mysterious leech-throb took control
    and sent everybody back to bed.

  it was the first of forlorn june. from mud
and the moist soul of a dead introvert
    they were born: the burst and bloom
of late daisies, lackadaisical lazies
    —a **last** spoonful of **memory**!

before the artistic syringe **of** experimental hate
and **agony** was injected,
   the literary tool of antipathy was inserted
   between them loose sheets of our digital
   time-lags. obtuse brain-rags **we** used to shed,
   then call a "sober fool's bluff," an "off-the-cuff thread"
   —till the aforesaid
   psychological molting was suddenly
      no longer **permitted.**

the transfer

that evening, i wasn't more
than a random blob of twinge.
a simple neural sore,
a decomposed cell-cripple.
by ten o'clock in the morning,
however, i became
   —through digesting the quantum-core
  of his perishable **shell**—
the whole organic stuff:
i was him, undeniably!
h**is** entirety,
rough and **raw** entity, chose me
through a chromosomal referendum
to be mine. mine, truly.

  "i'll be kind, mon chéri,"
i laughed into his acoustic hole,
auditory well,
              as his **awareness** withdrew

        into his right knee.

the existence

and thus began my metaphorical journey on paper.
onto it my memoirs had been written (apparently)
   —half **poetry**, half constitution
of a newly founded state of mind:
shattered pieces of a blind,
aberrant self-image with sharp edges.
sharpened then blunted by the numbness
of my heavy fingers, relentlessly
aspiring to hold onto the coffin nails . . .

come to think of it, it might've actually been the cold breaths, old
ghost-wails of my former, ideologically **deformed** host-children
that i was chasin'—constantly coughin', cradle-ridden they were
—until, one day, their lifeless lip-flakes stopped sailin'.

. . . then sharpened again through long,
arduous voyages from the living room
to the kitchen, as the soul's sails tightened
   —then in the opposite direction,
  as the spiritual erection wore off:
time to relax for a split second
before embarking inwards, to the visual cortex:

d'you see that miserable coffee-spill on the wall,
the fist-stain on the door i've got no words for?
they're the endangered entrance to the existential pain
we feel from this redundant cycle of hypocritical pretense.

from these allegorical excursions to remote,
undiscovered figments of someone's imagination—
where we acted as though we were the agonist,
or at least a subpar catalyst. certain uncertainties

would've missed
if we'd stopped—simply stopped to exist,
instead of dragging this listless body ahead,
   that'd been dragged too far already.

being missed—
what a heady sentiment we demanded!
albeit not to a degree that it would've
drawn too much attention
   (*even a certified hush might've sounded shrill, perhaps*).
for **the** crowds of sycophant clefts on
the fragile membrane of vital tension,
that so elegantly separates the universe
from its own parts and partial traits, are busy.

hence, they shan't be pestered with such a
trivial curse as this one. oh, they'd just
brush it off
   as another classic scenario of an **author**'s
mother-issued literary crush; itinerary-fissured,
litany-diffused dopamine rush.

the mother: prelude

*where the hell is **she**?*

lo!
trapped within this ink-dunked institution
of metaphysical vacuum,
just like the rest of us,

> celebrated by all
> *who matter and have any gravitas—*
> *in here, the axonal knots*
> *on our ontogenetic opprobrium*
> *aren't us unique*
> *as the mass-**produced***
> *hapax-legomenon-thoughts*
> *tend to suggest.*

it's only common sense!
much like the absence of matter,
the lack of gravity, and the zipfian-curved
pattern of our dance moves, disregarding all
definitions of elegance—hence, *it's quite*
*a pity when **this reality**, described as*
"bedlam,"
"a mad world, indeed," by many a vocal seed
of our feared lord, turned out to be
the very result of a bad beard-day,
a writer's-block-inspired conspiracy.

> rather similarly to:
> *when you look at this twisted madness*
> *standing on your head,*
> *you might be led to believe that*

"dad, i don't understand.
hobbes vs. locke—what's the difference?"
could meet with: "i'm sorry, lad. let me stop
the clock and explain everything afresh,"
   instead of the cliché sobs programmed to
accompany the good-old lash and bash™
home remedy (belts and divorce papers are sold separately).

   behold!
   she was trapped within
   this cog-operated bogus machinery
with me,
   where god's
   a brown marmorated stink bug,
   and zeros are constantly meant to be
   divided by the letter "a"
   for entertainment.

                  representing a sound i utterly
                  despised, but regretfully uttered
                  on so many painful occasions—
                  i just can't help myself!
                  especially when it **could've been**
                  avoidable with great ease, when it
                  shouldn't even have been part of the
                  syllabic yelp—the verbal wheeze-sandwich
                  i put in my mouth from inside out.

   still,
i chose to chew and then spit them
nasty expressions south- and sort of
westwards, with as many open front
unrounded vowels as i could possibly
cram in there, for good measure—

to the verge of risking
quite **a misunderstanding**
on sleepless mornings amidst
yawning owls and dry lilac towels.

*and oh, how dry they've been
without a wet dream about
the unknown, the unseen . . .*

the i: prelude

suddenly—*wow!*
it burnt my throat like a thousand suns.
the realization struck me: **i was** no more
than an average oxygen molecule,
   inhaled intensely
on a planet where i should've been
the atmosphere itself. where i could be
the tree of life, i was nothing but
   the apple of her eye—
a mere freckled fruit reflected on the retina.
a drop of sweat on a **stranger**'s forehead,
a globule of semen on one's foreskin—
whereas i imagined my role **to** be no less
   than the struggle,
   the inception.

the climb up onto an unmountable cliff
assembled there by **myself**.
   what a fate . . .
to be demoted to the stratum of tablecloths
protecting precious wood from getting
contaminated
   by some unstable clots, awful clot-drops
slowly oozing out of a full bottle of preprocessed
cosmic doubt.

an ornamental object,
a lonely ember of indirect ridicule.
an overslept cocoon i was to unplug soon
   —in their eyes—
swept under the oriental rug.
weighed down by a sepulchral vase

   wherein they placed a vaseful of their abominable ways
      and vague lies,
   instead of the traditionally wise choice
   of a wasteful flower arrangement.

   to hide the voice-tide
   and the denigrated bug in the castrated system:
   the poe-remnant, absurd argument
   that could've bent their leaning tower further.
   would've sent the foul taste of
   what they suggested by
"civilization"
   right back to the architect of this sadistic soup
   —the krotovukha of khlystic loop.

the mother: examination

    was she inconsequential, godforsaken?
    was she something, **or was i** mistaken?

i was achin' to give a response,
provide a logical explanation;
my host, on the other hand,
preferred to feel a strong urge to slap himself
    on the knee,
in a characteristically self-defining
and -defying fashion, in order to
conspicuously invite the audience
to witness **the sad result** of his external (attempt at)
        introspection.

a dull collection of lizard remains
was pointed out by the hard toenails
    with marred smiles,
hanging on the wall—exhibited proudly
in a splendid little case with a cracked glass cover,
through which a warped echo tickled
the deaf ears **of their** unborn offspring.

outside, december drizzle whispered
unethical secrets to umbrellas
stretched out above altercations.

    and romantic anecdotes
advised blushed cheeks, craving for
a flaskful of **goodnight kiss**, to sink
their shivering teeth into the wintry zephyr.

the "time"

time felt like a cloudy substance,
passing by and above me,
beyond my reach with the speed of a reignited flame
    —a lousy long-lost love
burning through each chamber
of the overly tame heart. days seemed like hours,
and years like minutes.
weeks were reversed and versed extemporaneously
to illustrate that, at this rate,
there'd be no return anymore to anything relatable:
i perceived the seconds
flowing in the veins of memories
we yearn for, as ordinary mosquito bites
   on one's shoulder.

as peculiar moles on gradually colder faces
that were partially covered by my hand
             —to reprimand the grime.tmp—
for i didn't want to taste their disappointed
blend of sour sound-slime and canned kindness.
such irksome actions provided the sole ointment
for my chronic lack of confidence
in the social-contract-borne sickness
that i couldn't recall i'd ever contracted.

   decades disappeared
without a footprint on my hippocampus,
yet the hereafter looked utterly mint and detailed
—i was a tainted tint of a prophet,
licking the feet of angels,
who simply needed to organize his neat visions
using dainty divisions and divine delusions.

there **i hoped to find** a clue—
the propulsion necessary to tell life
   and death apart.

still, to my regret,
i couldn't at all distinguish the two.
you see, for me:
   mortality was a whimsical cat tail,
   wagging left and right.
   a broken clock's large hand,
   oscillating epileptically between
     "it's a date then" and "sorry, i'm late again,"
   as though it mattered whether
   it was 2:27 pm or 2:28 am.

from the perspective of the twenty-seventh minute,
there wasn't much to do about this mechanical mayhem
—this infinite samsara it got sucked into.

   and now stuck!
for eternity **in** this ironic atemporality;
at least as long as our absurd desire persisted
to count down till **the last** feast,
leaving nothing but pitiful **crumbs**
and a half-dead wife behind before checking out
(**of life**, as well as the local breakfast and deathbed).

the "the"

                                              the?

                  the!

                                                              a(n)?

      the . . .

the mother: re-creation

what could explain her behavior,
    manner of existence?

serious endeavors were made to squeeze
a hint out of the undue deeds of an unspecified,
potentially nonexistent person, who might've
been the very glue keeping **my survival** intent
    intact.

was she a reluctant resident of my twisted
imagination too—materialized whenever
    i folded a chair or two?
was she**, in fact, a** rare metabolic **disorder**
anthropomorphized without her consent,
and thus given a status and a label on a lonesome
autumn night several years ago? i couldn't care
    less
about the probable psychological causes and
clinical sources of her essence—i simply referred
to her as "mother," for she was (in a comparative
sense, at least) the epitome of mothness. more
so than any other particular moth i'd ever been
lucky enough to get acquainted with.

her subliminally prominent presence impelled
me to hyperventilate and lose consciousness.
then later, i'd vomit a plethora of winged insects
    into the toilet
that made a familiar sound when flushed:

my father's rasp, wet raid scolding me each **time**
i mistook various pieces of furniture for a maternal
look—having dressed them up with assorted rags
   found on the street.

which begs the question:
  what's the proper prop, appropriate methodology
  that could embody her distant heartbeat?
    an arrhythmic ant colony, or an infatuated month
  spent on studying the **archaic** *methods of*
                      cardioscopy?

the father: prelude

by the way,

"she doesn't want to be around anymore;
you need to let her go, son," father warned me.

"no, not until the day i feel ready to cope
with **this** loss."

ergo: on numerous occasions,
   he caught me trying to have meaningful
   conversations with a **discolored** picture of the pope
   mother ripped out of the biweekly newspaper,
   buried deep amidst the cozy layers of garden moss
   and an old fur coat.

   yes. she felt remote.

"closer, come closer," i whispered,
yet no imagined movement answered
my desperate call. and no movement
meant more spur-of-the-moment,
fall-inspired, sonnet-like dread: was she
already dead in the physical realm (see p.57)
   and expelled from the immense ocean of
dense soul-lotion too?

   for the time being, she was still **everything**
      —as round as a circle can be,
      and as angled as a square could ever
      aim to become.

"in case you care: as it turns out, she's been
the long-antlered shadow of every tree all along.
each distorted shout and scream that wake us
from a bad dream full of pill bugs, to remind
their morbid throng that oh, what if they're
not   just wrong, but utterly so?"

he shook his miserable head, sweaty and
tear-stained from all the sad, low-bowing among
other melancholic mourners bowing even lower,
mopping the sweat-covered floor
with their carefully arranged hair. around
the deranged slow-dancers gyrating to silent
          despair here   and there,
tripping on alcoholic   void   and bare wire
—as they must.

"listen, son," he began again,
humming almost imperceptibly
the ten commandments—then upon
having added eleven more, he ran his fingers
through the smoky air and tore a piece off
for everyone to see: "where the hell is she?"

i cried when he raised his empty fist,
as if implying that her molecules weren't
—anymore—
included in this particular mixture of midnight
mist and wafts of sobbing breaths, puffs of breezy
   folklore.

overwrought to remove his socks, he
collapsed right in front of me, as i interrupted
this tragicomical scene of plight, misery, and
     chardonnay:

"nay. she isn't gone or lost, gathering dust
and rotting away in a wooden box—trust my gut.
quite the opposite: her spirit, ungathered dust's
dismay, remains in me and you. can't you feel it?"

  i spat 'em words as i saw fit, as they occurred
  to the grains of thought slipping through raw
  meat, swarming southwest via the venous
        v   i   a   d   u   c   t
  stretching ever so splendidly over the venomous
  valley of my emotionally inane mess.
  nevertheless, no textbook example of
  double-denial could alter the past: eventually,
  i had to confess.

the subtle head-shakes he made
  at my daily crusade against recognizing her
    irrevocable unavailability did
nudge me
to take one wobbly step toward a faint
sensation of acceptance. to my greatest grief—
and to father's relief, who'd grown admittedly
weary of my unrelenting effort to prove that now

    she could finally be

                        anything.

the universe: wounds

the sum of intersections . . .
even rough representations of a lettuce
leaf in the **microscopic** reverie of a butterfly
    i discovered not too far from our house,
exhibiting a somewhat similar personality
to his late wife's. it wore the same shade
of purple too, as mother used to on her neck
(in a rather extravagant manner, *if i may
mention*—on nights out to the opera, with
its thematic intention of domestic violence
and unsuccessfully muffled
    sopranos)—which also bore a coincidental
    resemblance to one of the most vivid hues
    displayed so artfully on my back and elbows.
visible only to me in the oval mirror that
happened to be the waxen window
    into the fatal error of plagiarism
        father repeatedly committed—for there wasn't
        anything unique or creative,
        really,
    in the way he painted his abstract murals
on my skin.

except for one thing, perhaps: in the
    absence of brushes and other conventional tools,
    he sufficed to use sheer force augmented by
        knuckles and buckles, his undocumented **fear**
    of remorse—or occasionally a fork that left intriguing
    marks on my otherwise optimistic aura. wriggling
deeper,
deeper, and yet deeper,
    with such a temperamental torque that the

benign barks of defense mechanism grew
therapeutic thorns, and the mild mystique
surrounding my condolent kernel developed
a wild temper through shedding more
irrelevant-looking layers of barks and tears.

these quadrifurcated wounds eventually wound
a millennium of painful todays around the
bound-to-cloud-eight fate (the economy-class
    equivalent of nephologically defined happiness)
of fragile yesterdays
that, less than four hours ago, still **dominated**
our docile ways—barely barked at, or tried to
tear through the flimsy membranes of time.

   now, though, my guile brain's ill.
such living works of art fill me up with—well,
   not surprisingly—an itch to kill what makes me unwell
    and the smell of sweet cherries, which mother would
    always mimic bringing home from the market, with
    playful larvae burrowed inside the flesh. quite appropriately
illustrating how i myself seemed to be responsible for ruining
the fresh finish on the feeble public façade of their abusive
masquerade:

thus, our household of a dozen derisive revolutions—
    manifolds of maligning generations—began to
    diminish, to fade. or so i was told.

   having
stumbled upon a set of forgotten ancestral
spoors, however, i followed them without
much thinking. without counting to ten,   off
    i went, along the offbeat, softly bent path
    tracing epigenetic tags hidden behind patches
    of grass—or sporadically right under the swollen

sole of my suntanned feet.

not to become like
   him, one by one i plucked them, collected the
   petite specimens into plastic bags destined to
   be discarded once i reach a dead end: the very
veil which used to interfere with my back and elbows
that bled to no avail. having understood the unfortunate
affair though, i just stood there. at the threshold, i froze
into a frail silhouette, waving goodbye to my voiceless
   wail.
   "cleave, sail away," i let the cantankerous cry leave
this lie-laden lair of my cold romance,
on-and-off flirt with the dirt-planet
     —*'til you're bold enough to return.*
   when the burnt-out world feels old
   and rough, i know you'll try, my tough love,
   to crawl back to me and earn my trust again!

my *rogue tongue, scathing monologue—*
now that we're apart, somehow everything
looks wrong and even the wrong's blamed
in vain.

   as you see, i'm all sore and stiff from the mangled
   temporal membrane you tore. hence,
   as i reunite with other runaway neural functions
   of mine, we might still feel a bit tense.
   but fret not, my phrenic
      (in its pre-diaphragmatic, greek meaning)
   friends: an opportune timing shall arise.

   when the sulk of anti-pyrrhonism is gone, and stars align with
   the clockwork of our **scheduled** *demise,*
   we'll devolve and become blind, compliant—
   tongue-tied once more lest we collide with

*the pliant lore of another mind
that doesn't mind the mental murk,
the unsanitary insanity.*

   to resolve and erase,
at last,
from memory the sock-obsessed **lunacy**.

the father: postlude

previously hugged by compassionate arms
that yet father'd stricken implacably with
his imperceptible charms—so obnoxiously
reeking of intoxicated rage.

   as if to wage a nonsensical war, simply to **regret** later.
   to soothe the panacean pain, to solve the mythical
   equation of lifeless life with the square root of acidic,
   quotidian brain-drain into the oarless seas of
     logos-free ouroboros.

   in delirious defiance against the mute cosmos,
   for creating the passionate possessor of such a
   preposterous lust-rust, and equipping him with
the must!
     the obligation to age. with the utmost ominous
     capacity to feel: the need to possess and reduce her
     to past tense—along
     with the weight of a redundantly harrowing
       existence.

he **would've** almost certainly stomped, treaded
the last drop of blood out of his own callous heart
too, if he could've
   —that is if it hadn't been a hollow
host for an artful arthropod. a faustian outpost, which
was to be relocated before the main thrombosed
chorus: only, out of boredom i guess, a rather curious
susurration from within the chest cavity became less
seldom and turned into a furious murmuration

one
fateful night,

as his tenant's rhythm-flock—mistaken for
a cardiac arrest—sought freedom
all of a sudden. to flee this flea-dome: a block away from
this hidden thought-, suppressed emotion-ridden
semi-cadaver, while i performed cpr to the unbidden
tempo of a far-sounding beat. to my brainwaves'
broken repertoire that riled me up:

in the heat of the moment . . .

i began to crop, cut, and chop!

a spontaneous notion of thoracotomy made me
act out of spite, whilst mother—who happened
to be taking the form of a fault-finding insight
sitting on an aliform stool (covered by one of
our finest embroidered pillowcases)—
insisted that i wouldn't have the faintest idea how
to squeeze the biting billows of childhood
trauma back into their birthplaces, and dying
fathers into melodrama-burdened embraces.
kneeling on top of him though, i was at ease
—as subtly so as his opined chronic disease—upon
having triumphantly released the prisoner
he'd **kept** behind bars of his ribcage for many a decade.

the rage was gone,
the deal was sealed—
and the uncaged, slightly outraged beetle
was finally free to depart, carrying a parent's
dismantled struggle into the **dark** lower-left
corner of the polaroid taken a few **hours**
later, by the ever-enthusiastic, photographically maladroit
coroner.

the mother: re-evaluation

an insipid insight was pronounced
dead on sight—the goose-feathered
minaret of confidence-steroid was, too,
apparently destined to collapse at some point.

through trial and terror, mother must've
understood that even her own trivial satisfaction
might
eventually
start to brood over the abrupt, yet entirely
foreseeable turn of events she'd witnessed.

  set in motion millions
of years ago, when god scratched his
constipated black hole and the panoply
of our tragicosmical atoms sprang out
of there in a world-quaking big bang
    of explosive diarrhea—leading to that whole
    shebang of morbid **curiosity** mixed with a trace
    of paralyzing rancor.

in reality,
  'twas nothing more than
    a tinge of tingling vigilantism,
an impromptu act of violently lifting
the ancient anchor of self-justified parental control—
  the queen of moths was still somewhat,
    somehow pleased sub rosa
by the obscene patricidal scene i'd **created**,
accidentally orchestrated as i helped her up
to her four wooden hooves then went ahead to realize:

she was but an empty roar of **nostalgia**.
   a glitch. a rotten ruse that couldn't quite amuse
      —*of course. what a bore!*

    such a nasty nausea.
      try to remember that.
      and grasp!
      hold onto

    the untold, warp'd echoes
      of now,

         even if . . .

the emotion

time flew like a disoriented wasp. in sharp
zigzags at times, or
   fancying rounder maneuvers at the most
   unpredictable points along its suicidal journey,
     heading towards
   a mortal collision with the hinges and joints
   of our universe—an indelible pen-plunge into
   the lonely **memories**- and mesmerizing
   hereafter-tales-flavored broth.

i naively aspired to eradicate both **from** my
tired garden of cardiovascular mementoes,
whence each
sentimental plant grew   and expanded.
   some wilted then rose from their dead—some to
their tiptoes
   to reach **beyond** the central rose-head and its
   hefty corolla, deposited with scores of saturated
   feelings, leaden with unwinnable battles.

   misguided,
sleepy
sleepy
sleepy
   chauvinistic chores.

        in order to breach the
blood–brain barrier, then bravely bleach my
gray matter before it could
beseech emotion to   step aside—
inculpate and vituperate, even   and worst case:
decapitate the cardinal carrier of adolescent

panic attack, and every cherished flashback
demanding their flesh back, pretending to be
ebbed away just to delay **the inevitable** crack
on their unremarkable shell made of reminders.

pathetic prompts to make us remember the
rancid decay
   —but hey, they're long lost now to this
   cerebral guillotine i represent. platonic
   cataracts no longer long for impermanent
   penchant. instead,
   they're replaced by logic and indifferent
   differential equations that're meant to
     (and they'd better)
   figure out how eternity's become
         an instant—
   the beginning of the everlasting intermezzo,
   the juncture in this epic tale of poignant
emptiness.
where we shall unite in an exquisite amalgam
   of amnesic comorbidities until the painful
   puncture on the quantum canvas—and
         through
that the extramundane atrophy consume us
in a stoically cataleptic fashion.

              yes, unless:
a self-centered session of subatomic saturnalia
   celebrating our future futility or past pity
changes
   our minds;
   rearranges the spiritual tumors growing
   on our malnourished nerves, as well as
   encourages us to act according to certain
   rumors: we're both fiction and fact!

*thus we're not better or worse than the
silence and tremors of what tonight's
supposed to provide under the lack of
moonlight. such fray and fright might   sneak out
as polite interactions into the wild
metaphysical sections—far from the foolish phenomenon
of a hypothetical hope's birthright that
already sanctions our home:*

*to recreate rome, first we'd need to bite
through her internal carotid artery. and
as she **bleed**s out, we must welcome the numb ambiguity
back into this interregnum of thrombus
and dust, where our rusty contours don't
feel so lost—so stupidly alone—anymore.*

   should've (and certainly did), a dot and a hexahedron
     melt smoothly here—**into** each other,

                          without rhy**me** or reason.

the mother: wall

"cheers! here's to the thyme mother would
've **never** used to season the meals she dreamt
of making. to the misused clichés she never
particularly loathed; the unwashed dishes,
uncleaned corners
    we all inhabited. no, **wait**—that's bonkers.
                  this is to creation itself,"
—*now i've got it,* i gulped and wobbled a bit—
"she felt that she'd failed **at**. conjuring up
decent human embryos impervious to her own
self-hatred was what she couldn't manage just
yet. the next **round** (*do pass them drinks around*)
goes out to the chemico-hormonal carnage we
were bound to consider sacred. to the ill-fated,
absurd groan that she'd feign to let us know that
she hadn't fainted. on nights we waited up
stranded—tending to her bland needs, **for**given her
   mammary gland for not being able to wrench   out
another droplet of nourishment for us anymore
   —not knowing, granted, that it'd all **end** up
   becoming, one particular darjeeling-brewed,
   seasonless even**ing**, the dull soundtrack to
our prewritten epoch. pinned with a yellow
thumbtack to

          a speculative wall."

the wall: mother

a wall that attracted the same flock
   of insinuated insults over and over again.
   they kept flying
   at us—   high
                     and low—as we wept, analyzed
in depth her
   random rue, projected onto almost anything:
   a bus passing by, a vulnerable housefly, or her
   personal stress-toy—the children. regardless
      of whether she truly believed that
   we'd turned out
   inferior to the phantasmagorical delusion
she lived in, we were still nothing:
   some blurry, eerie outlines expecting
      a **word** of compliment, at best
   —counting each curled clue
   (expectorating a world, a continent of discontent)
   as she hurled the **compressed**
   content of her pain-jar through forehead crease
   and lachrymal grease.

      observing the ptotic eyelids,
closed ajar on patchy
   hangover mornings—from afar, as skeptic surrogates
   for an antiseptic agent that could battle
      the anosognosic comeuppances,
      antagonistic side effects inter alia—
   we made bids.

i'd personally bet on **her**
successful recuperation
under regular circumstances;

although in certain instances, even i could entertain
the idea of some properly executed poetic justice.

when faced with our juridical anosmia, however,
nearing the summer solstice, we concluded:
keeping her dipsomania
and recurrent, convulsive calvinism
in check was in our best interest. lest
externalized vandalism committed on
her premo**to**r cortex should merge with
the omitted context—**an internalized**
contest of victim mentality that had already announced
checkmate on
her scarred **entity** and the circumjacent
potential of entitled scarcity.

for, in this gentrified jihad against
vapid sobriety, without our once-over,
why-art-thou-besotted-**again** scrutiny
—she was to signal the first wave of
martyrdom, per spiritum sanctum!

breaking   on the shores
of her mouth-to-rectum
donut hole, each rapid surge
of alcohol would've flooded
capillaries to purge every pore
of political incorrectness.

then later:

the i: birth

having dreamt less
    of her—of the flesh and gore,
the deoxyribonucleic acid and whatnot
   within her combustible core
   that willed the touch, created the
   sensation i was much used to
whenever i
attended to the soul-walnut she represented—
   i began to wonder a wicked lot
   about the birth i was tricked into.

    through fetal firth i alit sinned,
yet got acquitted
      by the digital dirt,
   beneath which
   the empirical rot would set in.
   where i'd itch. gently corrode away:

say, why on earth can't i be the reader or the writer?

why do i have to be the prey—
the to-be-slaughtered fay who endures all this
   literary trash, fey abomination.
   this sophomore rash. forced
slash rushed crash course on the
coarse reenactment of something
posing to be the emancipation movement:

"oh, miss 'er," they say, "but be remiss
and hiss at 'er like you mean it.
   sniff the meat-smell left on
      the hissed-at silhouette, then beat it.
it's the only way to heal grief,
to hear the pinguid peal of salvation!"

   thence arrives the need for a
   viciously vivid, yet lavishly languid,
   peer-pressured personification
   that's beyond the neural ration's limit
     —handed to me,

   when under the waxing gibbous
i came to be.
   as a heathen, born out of syphilis
               on the top of it;
yet my torn, obtuse spirit still couldn't stop
revolvin' around the haft-sin of nowruz and
    the bruise left by the initial half-sin,
    dyin' to be multiplied by fourteen.

from a whimsical womb that was,
   for all intents and purposes, the very
   quintessence of overprotectiveness
with
   hindsight-driven hints of gloom.
deprived of connate grace,
   of relief for an early tomb,
i was destined to bloom into another disbelief
mother could embrace.
            condemned to loom,
creep about in that empty, soporific room
of mushy muscle-cushions for almost five
months—wasn't my cup of euphoric doom:

so i crawled out!
victoriously in **the end**
 as a half miscarriage, half imagination
 of a rather poe-tick incubus with a soft spot
  for sophisticated torment.

 as half sewage, half inebriated furless being.
 i made it to the external skin,
  to the ever-thin membrane between
  fecal matter and the fetid, gin-permeated,
 kin-crammed attic air—*to be fair,*
i'd choose the latter on any given goddamn day—
 accompanied by
  the anglo-saxon way of compassionate
  carousing, frequent frowning
   at the obstetrical miracle that i was.

 they'd come **prepared**,
 i could tell somehow—ready for future frowns;
  and my posthumous delivery   to hell
was already prepaid and signed for.
  in the meantime, an antique kind of agony
 was waiting to torture me
 at every living moment: through
 the mental masturbations of an unrefined mind
  that's unkind to sentiment—
   to the nuances of experimental art,
   the many ounces of nonaligned,
   self-sabotaging emotions
   that now weigh down my tight heart.

and let's not forget about the agonizing
 effect of the most deranging dart:
 the bug-monologue in question
 that still went on (*oh, that subtle hum . . .*),
  elaborating ad nauseum on the precise

      procedure as to how one could fabricate
    a dysfunctional society and nurture numbing
animosity
      among its fictional members. to maximize
the entertainment value for all in favor
      of unsober surrenders and
      non-surrendering sober-ups
    that may jog but can't rush
      our drunken memory
    when it comes to inherited jeans
    and their butt-dialed calls: *hello.*
i'm a pocket, mother—
a fellow ghost-locket, spiritual socket
in a sense. let's communicate if you
    can be bother'd; otherwise, just fuck it.

soon 'twas the vengeful, high-ranking invertebrate officials'
turn to dance anyway—to shake a leg backwards, interject,
then burn explicit reports of gratuitous brutality against the
human race: unwriting our fate, reducing us to

curious echoes, gigantic chunks of motile flesh
   who can barely tie a shoelace to another
   without the classic
clash of pathetic parenthood and destabilizing,
     demoralizing individualism. *i'm out;*

away from the ludicrous coterie of
    laminated business cards and
    cardiac debauchery that used to
    anchor and make me say "thank 'er.
    thank god that she's fake."

                        which reminds me of

the sister: prelude

my ash-skinned sister,
>   while she was alive and awake.
>   all twisted and twirled, lukewarm like a lake worm,
>   who, during a game of anatomically confusing
>   twister, pinned me down and kissed **my** forehead.
>   then later, she told me that it was just a bad
>   **dream** i had—

to be a riven reverie, evidently, it did seem:
  i couldn't have been, the previous fall,
  the one who helped mother fall from a tower
      (52 meters or so tall).
    who made a capricious call to cut into,
    maul—as an infernal initiation, a perverted test
      —the very chest father **allowed** history to infest
      with water beetles of wrinkle and grasshoppers
      of gray hair.

>   an unnominated nightmare,
>   it had to be,
>   that accursed and
>   caught me in the atrocious act of strokin'
>   his scion's butterfly-bred bosom,
>   the ladybird-red lack of scrotum.

>   for which we both blamed god and his
>   patent-pending pet project: the sad **human**.
> afflated, evidently,
>   by a popular roach-rhyme broadcast
>   **to seduce** all the deity in that
>   segment of **infinity**—

"epicaricacy is the syzygy of
laugh, laughn't, and laughn'tn't,"
quoth the vehement verse.

the sister: birth

speaking of a misspent curse: two specimens
emerged out of father's unconditional, lifelong
desire to see the world burn,
become its own urn—in a hereditary, ash-free fire
that no oracle could've protested.

   and the second successful debacle
   manifested through the postnatal reek
of my dear sister:
      the cyst of all predicaments,
        forebearer of impediments, who'd laid
                           down
   the stone steps to the family crypt.

an anomaly she was!
having been born once yet left unsatisfied
   with the result—hence, she felt the need
      to reincarnate into a new nuance, hitherto unseen.
        a cleft of nuisance . . . a deft insignificance . . .
to beget herself again beneath quite obscure
circumstances, the not-quite-right stars: amidst
fraught silence, underneath the bridge of sighs . . .

without as much as a shallow attempt at a shrill shriek,
at de-winged whys while
     excavating the oxymoron that was herself
   from her very own uterus
             under siege by
mitogenic, reflexive hypnosis.

   convincing the self-fertilized fetus that she was
   to fix the unfixable and ruin the unruinable

   lest fibrous cannibalism be spontaneously
   triggered within **the** unstable composition
             of her organs—
  disorganized and eager to decompose at first,
  only to implode, and eventually   burst into
   a meagre bud—faintly lit by her halo,
   blinded by parental blood . . . lingering
    to be approached and baptized
by a hypermetropic moth
  scuffling to get inside through the window; whereas
  an invisible layer of sorrow-sown reality rendered
  all its spectacular travail so **pitifully** futile,
      so lamentably hollow.

  she was undoubtedly
  the most graceful plant out there; therefore,
  it was only fitting that, instead of the profoundly
  mundane outcome of lethal stomping by
some arbitrary passerby—*oh, and it was impending,
incoming already, at any moment!*—
  she was deliberately chosen
   for the honorable destiny of forceful relocation
   into her solitary pot-prison. deflowered,
  dehumanized, nevertheless infinitely proud
  of her status as a remarkable therapeutic tool,
  the vessel of constant resentment and
   childish fury of a be- then
   defriended fool.

  a gratifying sensation
shook her brittle leaves each time a litany
of blasphemies lashed down on her impure,
  unbotanizable body—corrupted by systematic
  cross-pollination, bestially polluted by carnal cravings
   and rueful **self-reflection**—
   as the fenestra to her soul was pried   open

and the moth
in question began to gnaw on the lampshade,
hitherto serving as the last bastion to blur
 her awareness regarding the dreadful fact that
  *she's nothing but mere words in a strange story
about insects and innuendoes.*

*and that her innermost insecurities
are to be exuded and diluted: out there,
 ridiculed publicly—leaving her withered and
 exposed to the savage judgments of society;
  to this arrogant apparatus rife with tarnished
  cogs revolving pointlessly in absolute disarray.*

so why didn't she shed tears of fear, or
 excrete pus of despair,
in the face of aforesaid feelings of humiliation—she
 wished to unwish. wished to un-unleash, even,
 upon her
 worst adversaries.
such degradation
that might've elicited—thus far unknown—past anguish
                    from her unconscious?

 *for she's an acanthus in a bolivian bowl
  that's already fulfilled its precious role in
this parable conceived by a simple anti-vertebrate mind:
  ultimately cast aside, dehydrated
and violated.
  maligned as typical mondays
  are passed over;
  as opposed to tuesdays,
   which are laden with leftover ashtrays*

                and unripe pears.

the i: eureka!

them crunchy fruits,
trench-coat-blanketed truths
would've surely been mother's obsession too,
if she hadn't detested
everything hard and rigid
that contained seeds: including, but not limited
to, her husband and father
—the latter particularly,
due to the undeniably detrimental
mental litter he discharged
into her undelineated literal **needs to**
cease to decease.

from my disease-perforated
perspective, she was neither alive
nor a**die**, however. until i laid my eyes upon
her respective soul-gates—
that is—and confirmed that she was
assuredly betwixt enjambed hadamardian states:
a nightmarish, dayharish
creature! contorted, unstable arrangement
of carbon atoms (*or athomases,
in case they'd prefer to keep it formal*),
seemingly inclined
to choose either abysmal
chasm off the opposing edges of
the mortality spectrum, ad libitum.

i wonder
if this schrödinger-esque ontological
mask was the subliminal source of my **life**long
post-somatic digress d**is**order,

    triggered each time i exerted the slightest
  amount of phalangeal impulse on
  typewriter keys—or forced inky remorse
into a ballpoint pen
  with such frightful ease
  that it penetrated the fragile hymen
  separating the internal and external void (rated
  three stars out of five
  by a random sample of seamen)
  —no longer keeping art and the
    turquoise sea pottery shard
    we found, apart. came across
at
rock
bottom
when an
old scar thought
to be a far phantasmagory
injured us again: percutaneous
bite marks bled, a tenuous telegram-
thread was blended with immigration
                laws getting amended.

to signify some misbegotten conceptions
of a comfort-zoned belonging.
just imagine the degree of
separation anxiety i felt
whenever i was zoom-
comforted to sink,
fooled into
believing
that our   kinkship

was ever worth more
  than the subtle epistemological
aftertaste of your upper lip.

(get a grip!)

*than a lump of fecal
waste, an eyesore of vomit-clump
on the bathroom floor that you clean and
clean . . . and yet you
still keep finding its irregular
remnants each time you admit: dammit!*

  *there simply isn't
   enough lack of linearity to our
dehumidified ataraxy that
could provoke even a vague sense of*

~~ephemeral unity~~.

the

#DIV/0!

the father: nostalgia

"a **fleeting** smile deceives every mile,"
goes the saying (*as far as i can evoke*),
then disappears in the distance, well-digested
by the hazy horizon. only debt and deceit, in
the form of paternal pain, remain.

he who,
    having hidden himself between the windowless
walls of his own brain's reel-racks—a complex
fungal hotel room with lawless, neural sex-stains
on the subcellular level: three bedsheets a day,
a couch blow-dried half the way, and
                  some droplets on the kitchen
floor—was simply looking for
   respect and affection amid
   the whole anti-artistic upheaval.

oh, what a bohemian whore! he'd never. never ever. fill that gaping
hole in his mediastinal core that i gouged out so willingly some
months ago—on new year's adam and eve.

   seeing him—the rubicund cunt—go,
the mortal fever retire
   from the coal-black center of his moribund
eyes made me realize anew. i felt that the semantic sinew in his
quondam wisdom had some weight again:
    "moan or groan in vain, you seldom notice.
   son, what you think you knew once is now   gone."
he blew a few smoke rings, then continued
exhaling his exiled teachings over another
fingerprinted glass of rum.

    "kill or die, it makes no difference from
    the point of view of the unborn, the hurried
    yet always-too-late conformist."
after a torn glance at the mysterious mist
outside, a clenched fist came down upon
the sturdy slice of apple-pied oak tree.
    "breathe or drown, it's a minor detail to the
    enlightened—occupied with choking on his own
    desire-free thoughts about the beauty found
    in the lack of lousy particles that may uncreate
    him and the rest of the world,"
crowned him, at last, his third drink, and
seventy-sixth slurred word.

the hour was late. each blink seemed distant and dim.
    no luck for an early bird—the suspected bend sinister.
    no flower for the unheard, unread writer.

    "and then re-uncreate him by the sheer
    power of true compassion that might unfuck
    his parents and make honey taste like bitter
    nihilism injected with the absence of dying
                     relatives' last breath,"
a stuttered teeth-clutch rejected all my default
definitions involving rapport and death—
    "in a selfless effort to negate civilization's
    tender touch on apish frontal lobes, while a
single teardrop
    secretly glides into the ear canal via primeval
    wrinkles."

    i perceived the opposite: the very deficit
       of such ancient aquaphobes
       —inside-out sprinkles, pre-irrigation ditches—
       on the bed sheet, which
         i dampened (*although it's really not my habit*

to piss and tell), and hurriedly
dried then shaped unhampered
to imitate mother's love-deprived facial characteristics.
to anger father (*i might as well*),
and confuse the readership—*as they presumably
still can't quite wrap their probabilistic linguistics
around the contumacy against dramatic irony:*

*being written about, yet wishing to stay unsmitten
by the romantic tension—defrost-*
    bitten by the lyric riot . . .

                                         be quiet!

the sister: time

*it's **time** for another poignant*
and thought-provoking question:
what, if anything, happened to the sister who was
systematically assaulted by blight
and canker? as fungi devoured her insides without
so much as a light-rail goodbye,
   she arrived at the insidious conclusion
   that she had to turn back time in order to emit kcab nrut
   —which sounded easy enough in her
   queasy head. when, however, rewinding her watch and
watching the springs unwind
   through her spanish windmill-twined,
   self-designed, double-blind-study-affined delirium-glasses
   didn't do the desired trick
   (*neither on the tick nor on the tock*), she understood:
a different collyrium was
   warranted here around the mycorrhizal third eye.

   thus **began**
her mad war against the
   gerontological why and all of its sinful accomplices,
   which, coupled with the semi-silent
   debut of dyschronometric disease, kept the family
   (and half the avenue) terrorized with
anti-temporalist despotism
   for almost a lustrum. she started by replacing
   most of the despised food past
   their prime in the gastronomic crime that was our
   pigeon-infested kitchen with fresh
plastic imitations—causing
   confusion and rampant ruckus on more than one occasion;
   for it took the poetry-poisoned

parents a few poultry-free weeks to espy the dearth
of polychromatic, post-digestive
    mucus.

to finally adjust to this
unexpected, parodical gastronaissant
change—that was
to chemically percuss a deranged range of their
lingual papillae—'twas this
    pro-synthetic interference that made the
    pmaternal pupillae dilate and 'em say:

    "wait a second."
the surreal west-anderson-esque—
    i reckoned—
east-coast-suburban-dust-after-a-school-bus-
sunset-scene-through-a-bird's-nest appearance
of their heuristic "oh"
was the very last straw:
the conclusive culinary steeple
poking them in the gallbladder,
foretold by the rather
unflattering phlegm-blur within the household—
    that the mold, and moldy, cold
        doorframes would've inherited.

at the market frequented by mother, ceramic
substitutes marked the crude commercial climax of
    what sister sold as a woke alternative to the
    pseudo-pharmageddon in demand.

    dear son of boke . . .
    who flew in from phew york . . .
    get the axe and end this joke—will you?

then came a period of a complete, out-of-the-blue defeat—as soon as calendars, dates on letters we knew not we had, and numbers we'd barely ever read—signifying the shelf life of perishables—lost every self-respected meaning. such a keen, relentless travail! to constantly alter what was written on each mail, on every single vernissage invitation . . . and in less than two shakes of a lamb's tail, we were at the reversed historical hem, at the very stem of sis'terical sabotage.

 —*damn, no time to tinkle:*
 'ere arrives our mirage-mangled,
 satire-strangled, human-mime tram!

the next station after the
 menological arrhythmia, logistical
 stone age, didn't affect the familia much. the good
 old twinkle of our native junction
 resumed its function—its dysfunctional defect.
  while deeply saddened by
 the inherent aptitude of minutes to fiercely
reject!
 retracing their steps.
eject! hours and days from their relapse-lent embrace.
 then (be)
deject(ed)! by
 the subterfuge of unembraceable, jetlagged distance;

 she decided to refrain
 from consuming food and be sustained by inner rain.
 by her waned brain-brood alone.
 and by prana, as the mood-motivated manifestation
of the final telomeric tone.
 in order to press pause on the peripheral torment she
  assumed to have originated
 from the temporal aspect
 of things—since she couldn't succeed in "the!" which

meant, indeed, in her dictionary:
"returning to the order of yore, **when** rivers ran freely and boars
bore less stress than humans experimenting with the missionary
mess. or at least a hundred years back, when
    there was more s'more in general,
    and a bit—just slightly—less s'less."

  and so on:
hence, her self-imposed
  inedia provided us with a
  well-deserved "nevertheless!" and a respite
  from the cruel "thus" that
  left right bright, and left in the dark—out of sight.
despite this fact, **we looked**
  in both directions for fuel: a frisson
  of furious froth that could soothe our hypochondriac
  stomach aches, and alleviate the infinitesimal
  intestinal afterquakes we sought to ideate.

(*a line or two more about her*)
  in case you'd arrived late to the author–
  reader rendezvous: no, she was never
out of fine tobacco,
  mixed with a pinch of dead skin from
    the caterpillar-thin, hemic callus of her industrious
    fingers, rolling the mother-knows-how-manyth
    cigarette of her vignette lifetime prior to the
    aforementioned metamorpho'sis into an
  immaturely pensioned, pinterest-featured
    plant-myth. through an ironic conflict of
    interest with fate, she became the tired drop
    herself—of paper-cut blood to sweeten this
    lung–nature reunion. then the carcinogenic
onion was ready:
  to molecularly belong.
  to be breathed into our akashic physiology.

what a pity that she had to die **at the** length
of one hundred and sixty-three, leaving a world   behind
that didn't have the faintest clue of what
our preview-furled,
pass-through life meant—or what it truly entailed:
a lamp got turned off.

what a fathermocker, damp waft-cloth!
all cloud-like and whimsical was her rough,
uncanny flow of ectoplasmic energy.

did she ever exist? was her existence ever enough?
a light bulb unscrewed, a fist unclenched: **past** tense was having a laugh. the medieval, unpasteurized twist of destiny settled the score without much of a fight—only a flock of minuscule regrets kept circling overhead. whilst a squalid school of poor decisions that weren't made did **and** didn't float underneath the empty bed— the whitewashed sheet she once occupied and covered herself with.

which is how i knew that she'd **lied**:
    in the very end,
        she did tame time.
        in a sense.

she did. emend the routine of tempoetic grime.
disrupt the sublime.

erupt into an elongated protein sequence:
a proto-enzyme of esperance!

and through a diary entry dated −85y,
it dawned upon me that her auto-annihilation

        —although it wasn't exactly the kind of
confirmation or quasi-firm notion i was in quest
for—at least answered one single question:

can we ever climb this ephemeral hill,
   beat this epochal beast completely?

"it's half past past. still: shedding their last thinned-out layers of twisted skin—the bygone years. with bent rays of nonlinear arrogance, they surround the glass-crowned dance of our lonesome days to come."

so no. the answer's self-explanatory:
   no ritual remedy;
   no serendipity rushes to our aid
   in this chapter
      regarding our age.
   the months, the offstage acts
      we're afraid of.
         the die. the alone.
            the off. the end of i.
      oh, don't cry, don't moan.
   remind yourself: mankind's a mean loan.

the mother: reference

   the **weep**ing willow looked at me
      questioningly,
   through the curtainless gap
     of saturated insincerity, commemorated
     by an esoteric palm print:
  the map of my qualm,
  the blueprint of my mishap.

   then it began—this sick,
    sobbing sap-stick—to sing to me,
     as per our agreement,
    even those taken-**for**-granted
promises she'd never meant to ferment.
              yet she did,
    by jealousy and not-
    quite-elegant premises—
  that's how **my foolish soul**
    tore its ligament from the shameful
    body, and got sucked into this
    figment of
  a literary black hole. as space bent, shapes went
                                      detour

  and colors blent without contour:
   our romanticized reality span
out of   control.

   some ran—the pedophile neighbor,
    the tile salesman—but alas, to
   no use were their
   aporic feathers
   against the righteousness
  of our (sagaciously sour, fully converted)

moth-fearing prayers.
these (*one can say,* fairly demented) chirping chants
   had such a pareidolic power
     (*oh, what a committed choir!*)
that it'd devour them—heretic interpretations—
   one   by   one.
   at the deformed church, no less—
which charges by the hour: the place of
whoreship for stepmothers, and that of warship
   for other place**hold**er stereotypes—
   we clogged their windpipes with "i should
   've told her;" won their heart chambers a
   son, a daughter at a time.

if ambitious
annexations were indeed a crime, how come
you didn't crimea
   *river, sing **me** a russian-dolled rhyme?*

   while i rolled and
   turned my cold back to mother's
     alleged demise. or w**as** she just
     asleep—constantly—never even
     unclosing her eyes?
   a cheap memorabilia, a
   parasitic paraphernalia she'd **mutate**d **into**
   by then—her agnostic atria and
       venomous ventricles
had permutated, too, according to
   the mad memories going through
   my head . . . *going through my memories . . .*

   so sad:
     life's wed death, yet
     neither could   undo
     this breath of bookworm birth,

cancel this between-the-lines
  earth where germ-like **words**,
    syllables like cancer, bit me on the very
    shoulder. whence, a rare prairie flower
    bloomed—with petals as vividly
      pink as mother's desairological
      lip ink.

and when that sip-sink sent a blink
    towards me, to tease my r.i.p. kink—
    a whimsical wank-wink to posthumously please?

    i knew the ultimate bell state:

was she al1ve or g0ne?
    and *am 1* the outcome—
    or just s0me cnot-loop drumbeat still on?

    limning a spillo'er syncope . . .
    the w1ll to cope . . . the slip to c0py . . .

either way, i'll remain—
  yours truly—
a schizophrenic relic,
a sip of paraliterary trope . . .

the sleep

nothing. to do. except: surrender? perhaps.
uncertainties woo me, render everything arbitrary.
insecurities take my mind-traps captive, tire out
what**'s meant** a thing once—no—don't leave the door
open to more distressing pen brushes on the floor of
this empty home that's supposed to gently whisper
into my ears monochrome phrases of tender verbal
embraces. which i adore, i itch to reach, no matter
the cost; whereas the truth is that i've already
lost the battle: the hassle of commitment i've sort
of dreamt of is barely lent, and not at all given **by**
the hidden entity who's driven me to this tall,
unclimbable freak of a tree in **the first** place. i've
tried to trace it back to the time i was cursed with
a **kiss** on the neck—by an inherent flaw in the system.
and even though i miss them, those careless nights,
the innocent fights over less than a cent—i'm here
now, to grow. to reluctantly show, to whomever
happens to tempt me, the rather pleasant side of my
anxiety. the relatively uneventful ride on this roller
coaster called astute injustice that'll lull me to
sleep in a minute.

www.ingramcontent.com/pod-product-compliance
Lightning Source LLC
Chambersburg PA
CBHW071415040426
42444CB00009B/2256